# Turner

## THE ESSENTIAL PAINTINGS

# Turner

## THE ESSENTIAL PAINTINGS

Valérie Mettais

**PRESTEL**

MUNICH · LONDON · NEW YORK

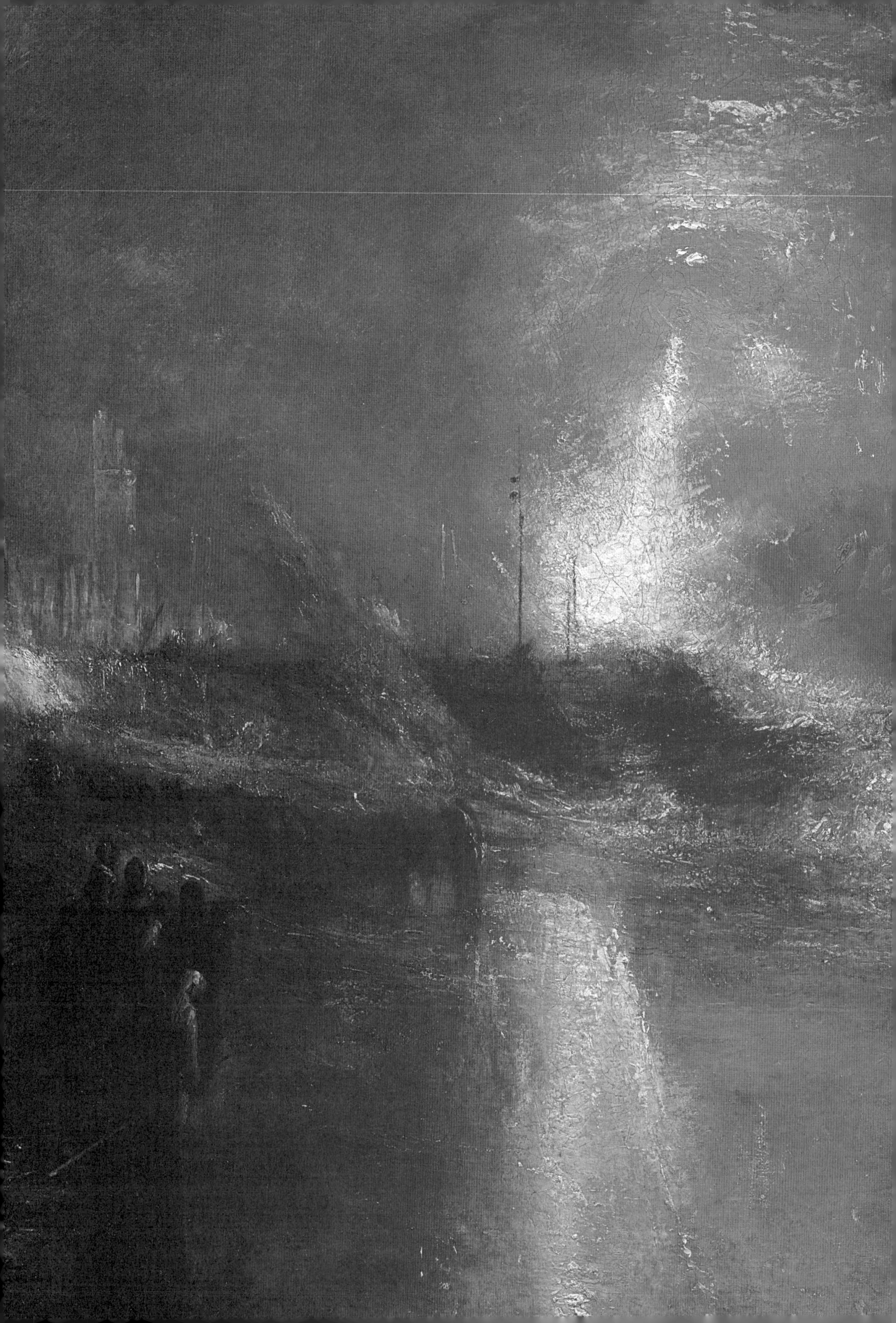

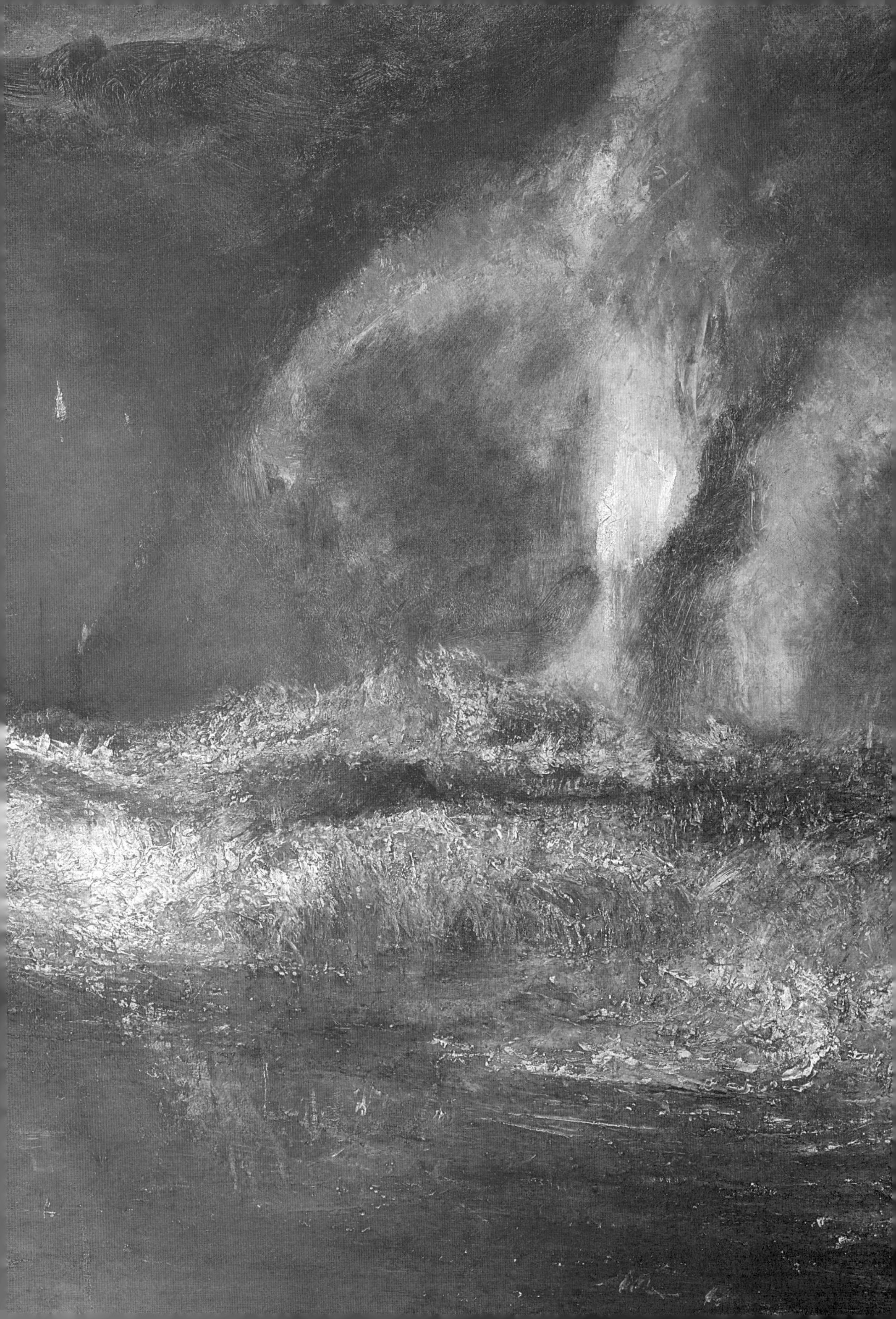

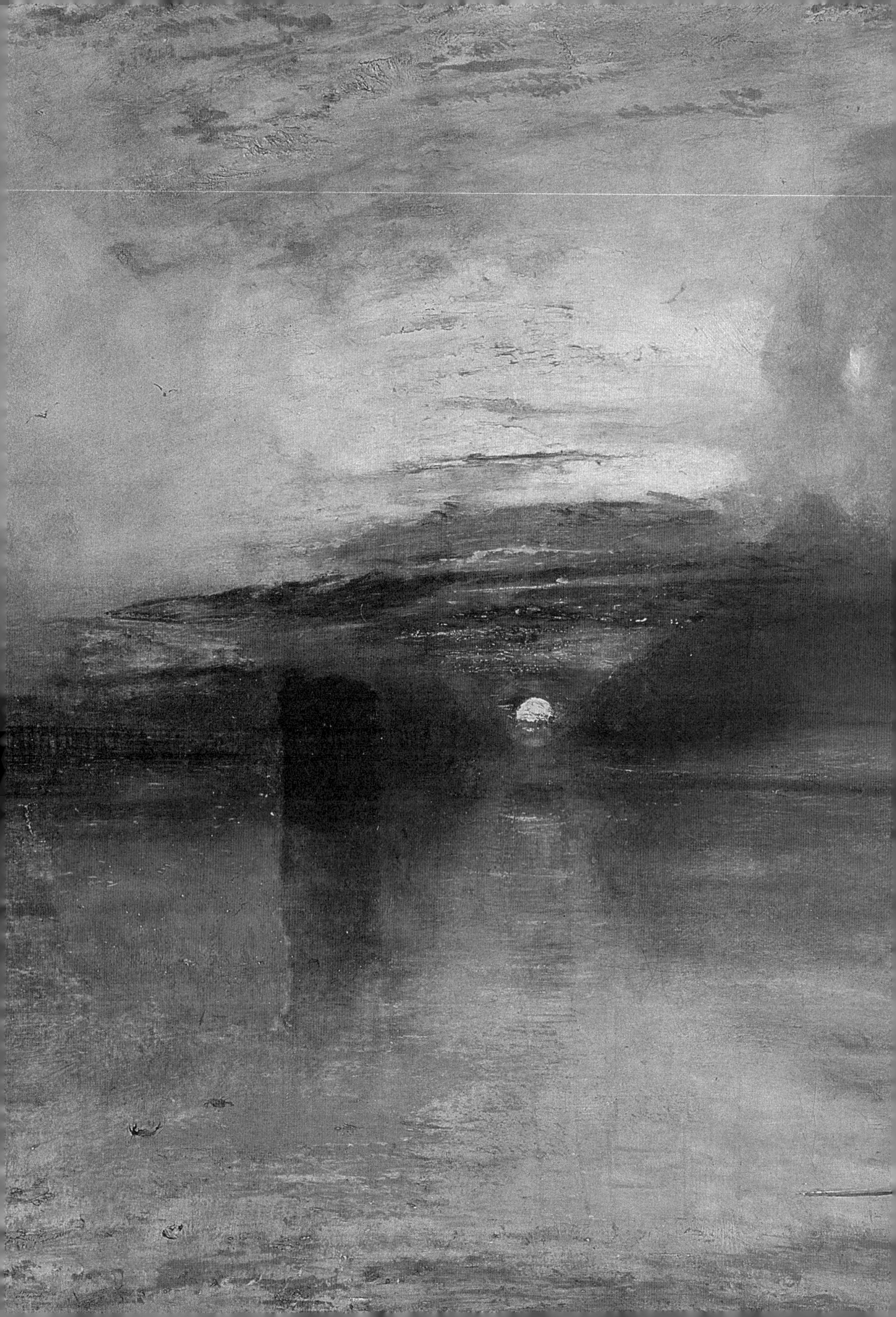

# Joseph Mallord William Turner
## (1775–1851)

*… Turner, who worked almost entirely with his palette knife, was observed to be rolling and spreading a lump of half transparent stuff over his picture, the size of a finger in length and thickness. … Presently the work was finished: Turner gathered his tools together, put them into and shut up the box, and then, with his face still turned to the wall, and at the same distance from it, went sidling off, without speaking a word to anybody, and when he came to the staircase, in the centre of the room, hurried down as fast as he could. All looked with a half-wondering smile, and Maclise, who stood near, remarked, "There, that's masterly, he does not stop to look at his work; he knows it is done, and he is off."*
– Edward Villiers Rippingille, at a Royal Academy varnishing day, 1835

Turner is considered one of the greatest Romantic artists of Great Britain, or anywhere else for that matter. Not only was he a genius watercolourist, a master of historical landscapes and a pioneer in the study of light; he was also extremely ambitious. Recognized very early by his peers, he achieved renown, financial independence and creative freedom as a young painter in the early nineteenth century. The intrepid Turner explored much of Europe. He was insatiable, adopting diverse inspirations and techniques in observation, composition, invention and the sublime ("delightful horror", as Edmund Burke called it in his 1757 treatise on aesthetics). He moved from oil and large formats to drawings in which he often eliminated all traces of humanity. His subjects ranged from storms, avalanches and infernos to battles, abductions and catastrophes, entrancing precipices and infinite perspectives, blue-tinged sunrises and the glowing sun, reflections and dissolving light. Without ever losing sight of these things, no matter how faint they were, Turner shared his experience of tumult, vertigo and awe with viewers.

# An Impeccable Record

*Mr. Turner is, indeed, a very powerful artist, and all his works indicate a strong imagination. Nothing little appears from his hand, and his mind seems to take a comprehensive view of nature … [but also] negligence [which] appears like affectation …*
– A review in *Porcupine* (London), 7 May 1801

To become an associate member of the London Royal Academy at the age of twenty-four was unheard of, but Joseph Mallord William Turner achieved it in late 1799 – and that was just the beginning. Born on 23 April 1775 in Covent Garden, he began drawing at an early age, and at fourteen he was admitted to the Royal Academy's school. He was the son of William, a well-known barber and wigmaker near St Paul's Church, and of Mary Ann, who came from a family of butchers. The lively neighbourhood had bustling boutiques and theatres. The young Turner copied the masters and coloured engravings for printers and publishers, and his father was so proud of his exploits that he displayed them in his shop window. Working on topographical landscapes for an architect, he drew home interiors, large estates and their surroundings in scrupulous detail. To this initial training Turner added diligent work at the Royal Academy following antique and contemporary models alike. He then perfected his vision, exhibiting a watercolour in 1790 at age nineteen and an oil on canvas six years later. His career was off to a roaring start, and the foundations were strong: detailed knowledge of the Old Masters and classical culture; a passion for Claude Lorrain, Nicolas Poussin, Rembrandt and the maritime painters of the Dutch Golden Age; the primacy of seascapes and skyscapes in the hierarchy of genres; the important role of the Royal Academy; an interest in the relationship between painting and poetry; and virtuosity with watercolours. Everything was in place. It was now up to Turner to be faithful to these principles – and to revolutionize them.

# Touring Europe

*Turner is in the neighbourhood of Naples making rough pencil sketches to the astonishment of the Fashionables, who wonder what use these rough draughts can be – simple souls! At Rome a sucking blade of the brush made the request of going out with pig Turner to colour – he grunted for answer that it would take up too much time to colour in the open air – he could make 15 or 16 pencil sketches to one coloured, and then grunted his way home.*
– George Soane, in a letter to his father, 1819

Watercolour was the medium with which he trained and achieved success, and this technique would accompany him as he travelled for decades and executed his large oil compositions that were exhibited at the Royal Academy and the British Institution. Upon his death Turner left behind some nineteen thousand watercolours, proof (if any were needed) that he was part of a British tradition which had been well-established since the eighteenth century but had seen notable developments in materials. Small, ready-to-use squares of paint were available to him; he could transport his implements in a box – or a hollowed-out bound almanac – and work on site or even in the evening, at his lodgings, after filling sketchbooks and noting down light values during the day.

Travel was an essential experience for Turner both as a person and an artist. It acquainted him with the extraordinary diversity of nature, landscapes, climates and weather conditions. He studied maps and guides, and he drew up an itinerary of must-see places. England, Wales and Scotland were among his first destinations. Then, in 1802 and from 1817 to 1845, he made about twenty journeys to Europe, most often in summer: to Switzerland, the Netherlands, France, along the Rhine and to Italy, among other places. Above all, he loved the Alps for their dizzying views, Venice for its light, Rome for its history and its artists, Paris for the Louvre and the banks of the Loire and Seine for their reflections.

All this travel did not prevent him from pursuing an exemplary career both in the art establishment and among sponsors and patrons, that is, aristocrats, merchants and industrialists. Following his promotion in 1802 to Royal Academician, or full member of the Academy, he signed his name "J. M. W. Turner RA". He exhibited when he pleased, and he became a member of the administrative

"

council and the hanging committee; he was elected the Royal Academy's acting president in 1845. In his Harley Street residence, he opened a gallery in 1804 to show his work directly to patrons, without restriction. He was named professor of perspective, and from 1811 he presented a series of lectures. Despite the critics who assailed his works, Turner received every honour imaginable and attained renown for his art and erudition. He often gave his paintings long, evocative titles, accompanying them with quotations or with verses of his own. A keen student of Greek and Roman mythology and history, he created immense, ambitious compositions on Homer, Virgil and the Bible, as well as on the fates of Hannibal and Regulus. A paragon of Britishness, he celebrated the national mythos, painting scenes such as the battle of Trafalgar and the final voyage of the *Temeraire*. A man of the nineteenth century, fascinated by speed and light, he depicted steamships and steam locomotives and kept up to date with research into subjects including physics, optics, chemistry and astronomy. He accumulated responsibilities and talents, but this academician, teacher, mentor, colourist, and painter of history and landscape also harboured poetic ambitions.

## The Indistinct, the Undefinable, the Void

*[Turner's face] is red and full of living blood, and although age has left its mark upon him
it does not seem to have taken his energy of mind, for this lives in that observant eye and
that compressed mouth, the evidence of an acute calculating, penetrating intellect, which
I may mention is seen in the whole contour of his face. He is a great little man – and all
acknowledge it. I remember old Cooper told me some time ago that when any of the members
of the Academy were "in a mess" with the effect of their pictures a single application to
Turner would put all right – he never failed and his words were listened to as the law.*
– C. H. Lear, journal, 3 May 1847

On the Royal Academy's varnishing days, spectators came to witness in person the spectacle that Turner would stir up. Before his colleagues, the magical painter would buff, polish, revise and finish his canvases, revealing his creations live before the eyes of everyone and joyously competing with his neighbours – particularly his primary rival, John Constable. At each exhibition, everyone talked about him. They went into raptures before the one they called "the painter of light" or "the painter of fire" – after praising his "brush of snow". All his life, the critic John Ruskin praised him. But people also mocked him as confused and offensive. When a sceptical patron found his painting "undefined", the artist sent word to him that "the undefinable" was precisely his strength. One notes his propensity for exaggeration, his extravagance, his affectation of carelessness, the way he did not finish things – or gave the impression that they were unfinished. Regarding the sunsets that consumed the composition, critics scoffed at Turner's "jaundice", and he certainly did make liberal use of certain colours. To William Hazlitt, Turner's pictures were "too much abstractions of aerial perspective"; he followed by writing in 1816 in *The Examiner*, "All is without form and void. Someone said of his landscapes that they were pictures of nothing and very like." This void would inspire more than a few artists in the twentieth century.

William Turner died, aged seventy-six, on 19 December 1851 in Chelsea, following a rather secretive private life and a very full public one. He had expressed one wish about his works: that they not be separated, as for him they made sense only when viewed together. Intent on organising his own legacy, he provided for everything in his will, particularly the founding of a gallery devoted to his body of work – three hundred paintings, half of which were unfinished, and countless drawings – and of a charitable institution for "male decayed artists, being born in England, and of English parents only, and of lawful issue". Turner is buried alongside his predecessors and fellows Joshua Reynolds and Thomas Lawrence in the crypt of St Paul's Cathedral. John Ruskin, the executor of his estate, would attempt to conceal the existence of many erotic works among his papers.

## And What a Legacy

*This man Turner, he learned a lot from me.*
– Mark Rothko, upon leaving the exhibition *Turner: Imagination and Reality*
in New York, 1966

What would Turner have thought of his immense critical and artistic legacy?
Would he have rejoiced upon seeing how many artists he had influenced, and
how diverse they are – whether or not they acknowledge him? Would he have
thought that was in line with his ambitions? Would he have rued the inevitable
and unexpected misunderstandings that would come about a few years, or even a
century, after his death? Regarding Impressionism, the story is well known: Claude
Monet and Camille Pissarro discovered his art in London in 1870. They used this
discovery in ways that are fairly clear. Berthe Morisot wrote to her sister Edma
from London in 1875, "I saw much of Turner (Whistler, whom we loved so well,
imitated him very much)". Indeed, the American painter James Abbott McNeill
Whistler engaged extensively with the "painter of light". In the twentieth century,
it became more and more widely accepted that Turner's works had caused funda-
mental change, thanks to many American painters including the most prominent
practitioners of Abstract Expressionism, from Mark Rothko to Barnett Newman.
In 1949 André Masson wrote, "Turner was ready to shake the confines of his
theatre, to push aside the porticoes and dissolve the frontiers of the sea." There
may be a divergence between what Turner wished to accomplish and the way
that some have subsequently seen his work, but what more beautiful divergence,
what more beautiful and richer reinterpretations could we hope for in art history?

# Further Reading


## Books

Olivier Meslay, Turner: *L'incendie de la peinture*, Paris, 2004. Available in English as *Life and Landscape*, New York, 2005.

John Ruskin, *Modern Painters*, London 1843.

Ian Warrell, Karim Ressouni-Demigneux, Olivier Meslay, Pierre Wat, Nancy Ireson, Stéphane Guégan and Laure-Caroline Semmer, *Turner: Ses maîtres et ses héritiers*, Paris, 2010.

Pierre Wat, *Turner: Menteur magnifique*, Paris, 2010.


## Exhibition Catalogues

Lawrence Gowing, *Turner: Imagination and Reality* (exhib. cat., New York, Museum of Modern Art), New York, 1966.

*Turner – Whistler – Monet* (exhib. cat., Toronto, Art Gallery of Ontario; Paris, Galeries nationales du Grand Palais; and London, Tate Britain), London, 2004.

*Turner and the Masters* (exhib. cat., London, Tate Britain; Paris, Galeries nationales du Grand Palais; and Madrid, Museo Nacional del Prado), London, 2009.

*Turner et la couleur* (exhib. cat., Aix-en-Provence, Hôtel de Caumont), Aix-en-Provence, 2016.

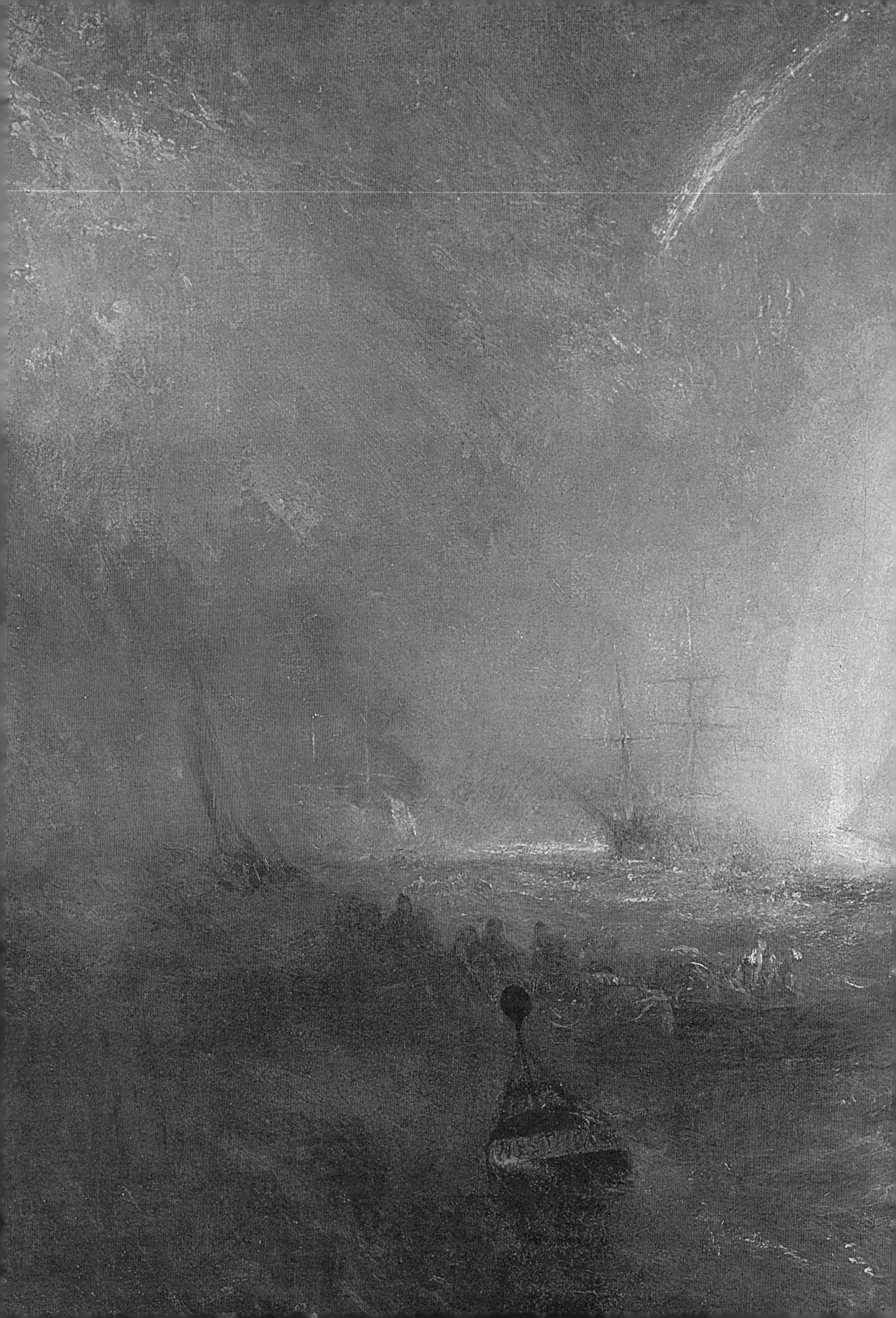

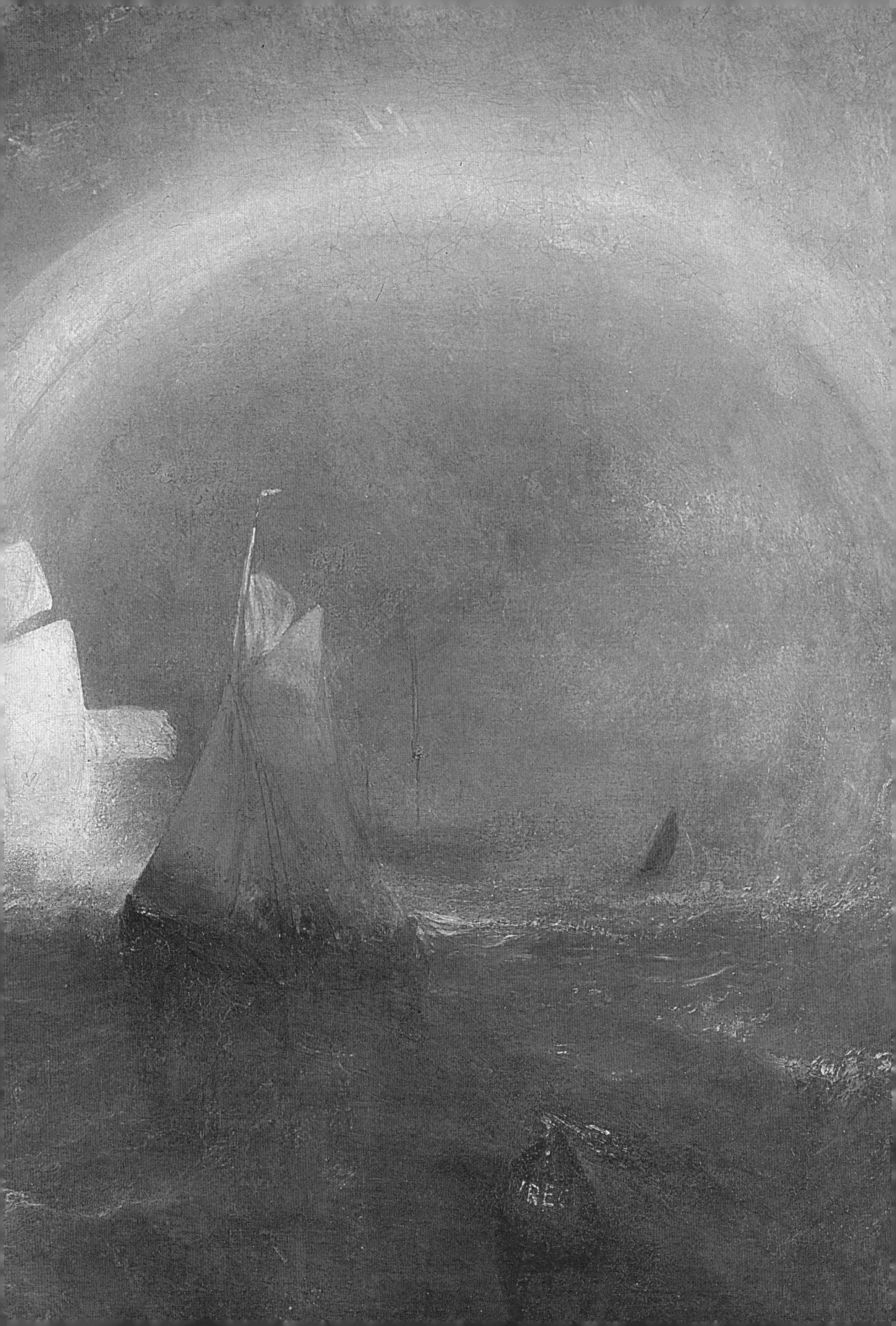

1 | *Fishermen at Sea*

This work, which is the first oil painting Turner ever exhibited, shows that he had already mastered the technique. The twenty-one-year-old artist met the judgement of the public and of his peers with calm: his artistic education, which drew from the European traditions of the seventeenth and eighteenth centuries, gave him the confidence to produce solidly constructed marine paintings with lighting effects and dramatic force. Near the rocks off the Isle of Wight, these vulnerable fishers, with just a small lantern, are guided solely by the light of the moon.

2 | *Conway Castle, North Wales*

Watercolour was at the heart of Turner's artistic practice. It was the first technique he used – with immense critical and financial success – and he would stand by it through all his travels, to help him set down his observations. He considered it an exercise, a step and a study, not a finished work. In his first drawings in the late eighteenth century, he aimed to recall sites and architectural styles. Graphite defined the contours; gum arabic may have been used as a binder for pigments or for coating the paper to which the watercolour was applied.

3 | *The Fifth Plague of Egypt*

In the Book of Exodus, it took no fewer than ten plagues to force Pharaoh to free the enslaved Hebrews: from water transformed into blood to frogs, lice, flies, the death of livestock, boils, hail mixed with flames and devastation (shown here), locusts, darkness, and the death of the firstborn. By depicting the seventh plague – not the fifth, after which the artist titled the picture – Turner chose a biblical subject for his first historical painting.

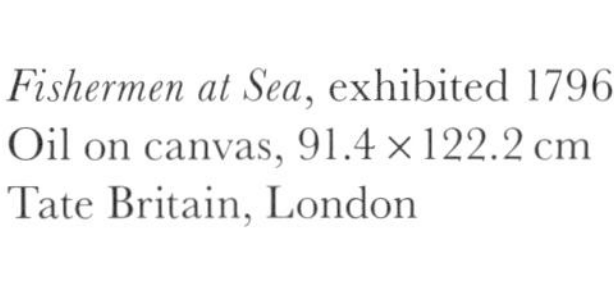

*Fishermen at Sea*, exhibited 1796
Oil on canvas, 91.4 × 122.2 cm
Tate Britain, London

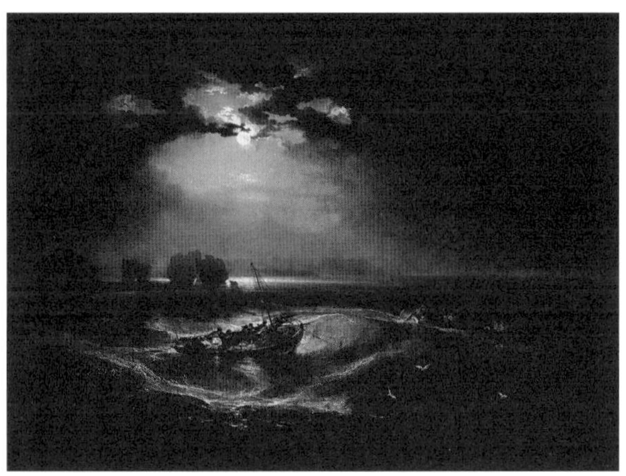

*Conway Castle, North Wales*, 1798
Watercolour, gum arabic and
graphite on paper, 53.7 × 76.5 cm
J. Paul Getty Museum, Los Angeles

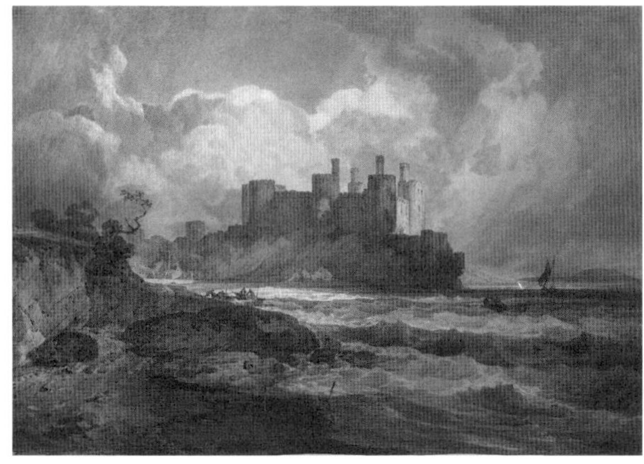

*The Fifth Plague of Egypt*, exhibited 1800
Oil on canvas, 124.4 × 183 cm
Indianapolis Museum of Art

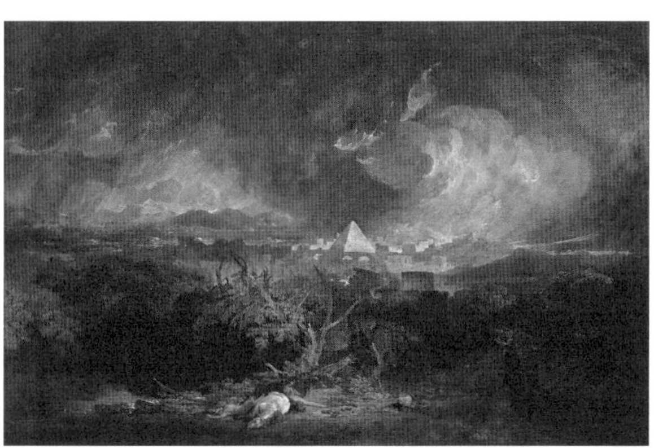

4 | *The Devil's Bridge, near Andermatt, Pass of St Gotthard*

Fascinated by the Swiss Alps from his first stay there in 1802, Turner would return several times. A bridge which appears suspended above a vertiginous void, mountains which had only been explored in recent decades, gouged-out slopes overhanging the void, a spectacular view of rock and snow: it is no wonder that a travelling artist seeking the sublime – that is, beauty steeped in terror – would be enticed.

5 | **Boats Carrying Out Anchors to the Dutch Men of War**

Pursuing dialogue and rivalry with the Old Masters, dethroning them, referring to and surpassing their lessons: this was one of the main aesthetic principles that consistently guided Turner. He scrupulously followed Royal Academy Professor Joshua Reynolds's 1781 recommendation on the seventeenth-century Dutch artistic tradition: "Painters should go to the Dutch school to learn the art of painting, as they would go to a grammar-school to learn languages."

6 | *Snow Storm: Hannibal and His Army Crossing the Alps*

Below, we see history, and above, a whirl of paint. Below, the Carthaginian general's troops in 218 BCE, during one of the Punic Wars against Rome. Above, the fury of the elements, the all-powerful splendour of nature. In June 1812, an enthusiastic critic for *The Examiner* hit the bullseye in his praise of Turner's sense of invention and terrible magnificence: "The moral and physical elements are here in powerful unison blended by a most masterly hand, awakening emotions of awe and grandeur."

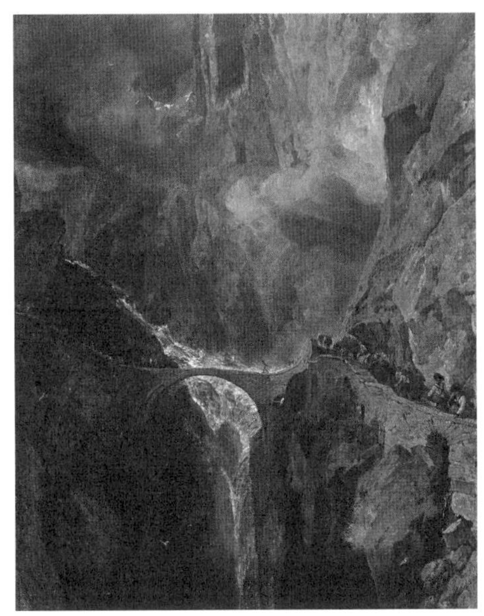

*The Devil's Bridge, near Andermatt,*
*Pass of St Gotthard, c.* 1803/1804
Watercolour and graphite on paper,
76.8 × 62.8 cm
Private collection

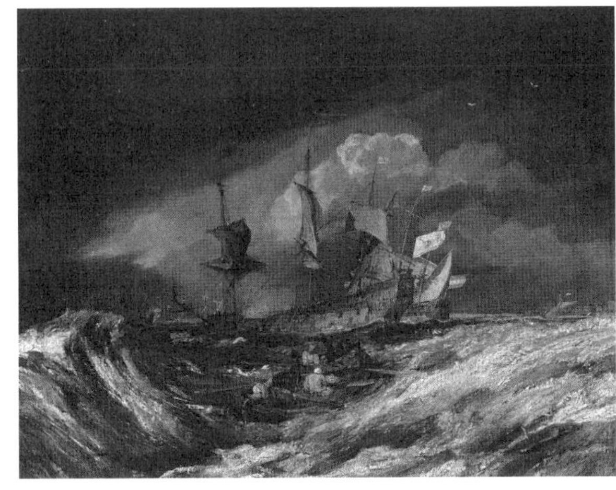

*Boats Carrying Out Anchors to the*
*Dutch Men of War, c.* 1804
Oil on canvas, 101.6 × 130.8 cm
National Gallery of Art,
Washington, DC

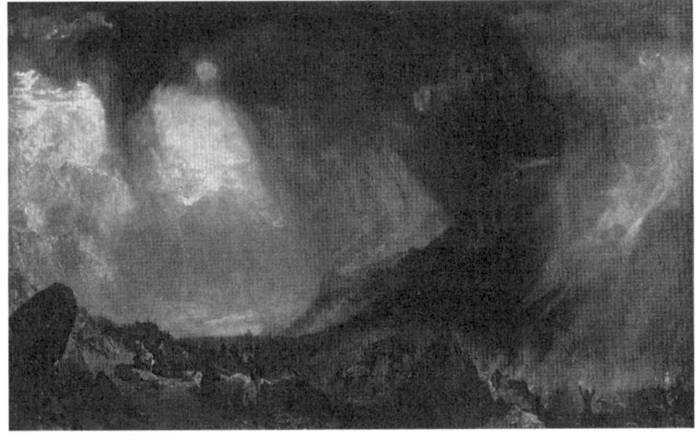

*Snow Storm: Hannibal and His Army*
*Crossing the Alps,* exhibited 1812
Oil on canvas, 146 × 237.5 cm
Tate Britain, London

**7 | *Lake Avernus: Aeneas and the Cumaean Sybil***

Claude Gellée (also known as Claude Lorrain, or "le Lorrain" in French) was an eminent seventeenth-century painter of historical landscapes, and homage to him is central in Turner's work. Legend has it that while viewing a painting by his renowned predecessor, Turner collapsed in tears, despairing of ever creating something comparable. Broad horizons, balanced compositions that play with serenity, great attention to light and atmospheric effects, and a mythological subject (in this case, from Virgil's *Aeneid*) – Turner took it all from Claude's example.

**8 | *Dido Building Carthage***

As she left the Phoenician coast – where her husband, Sychaeus, had been murdered – Dido, daughter of the king of Tyre, settled on the coast of northern Africa. There, she would found Carthage, the new capital of her people. Once more, Turner took his mythological and legendary framework from the Latin poet Virgil. He also borrowed, once again, from the compositions of Claude Lorrain, placing the scene in a grandiose setting, bathed in light.

**9 | *Vesuvius in Eruption***

For Turner, any natural occurrence that violently ran wild, overflowed, exploded, wreaked havoc, collapsed, blew up and sprung forth was a spectacle worth painting. All that shone, illuminated, deteriorated, reflected, ignited and turned all the colours of the rainbow was a luminous enchantment that Turner found worthy. As such, there is no chance the eruption of Vesuvius would fail to move him, even though he did not witness it. He worked from a colleague's drawings to compose it.

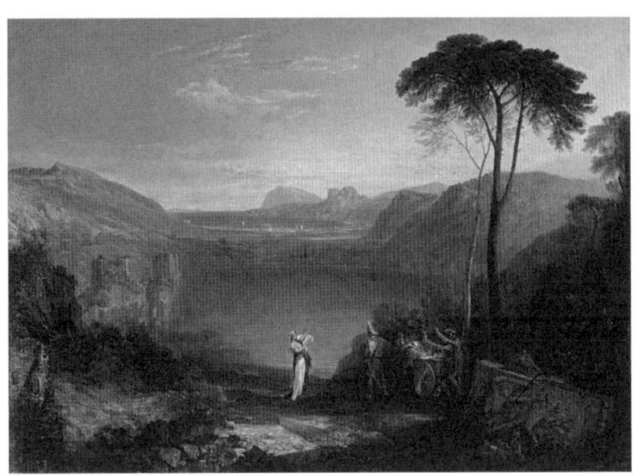

*Lake Avernus: Aeneas and the Cumaean Sybil*, 1814/1815
Oil on canvas, 72 × 97 cm
Yale Center for British Art,
Paul Mellon Collection,
New Haven, Connecticut

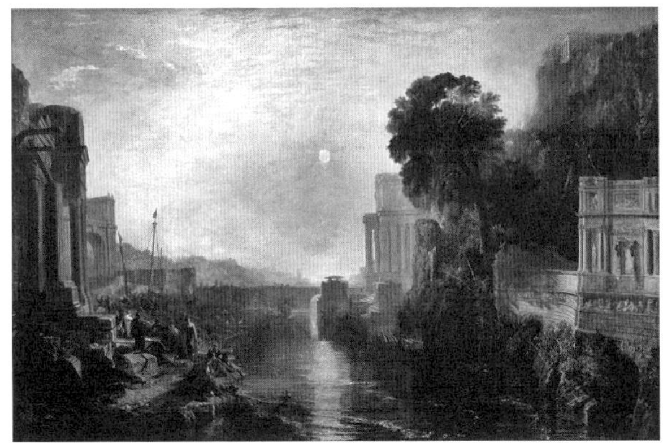

*Dido Building Carthage, or The Rise of the Carthaginian Empire*, exhibited 1815
Oil on canvas, 155.5 × 230 cm
National Gallery, London

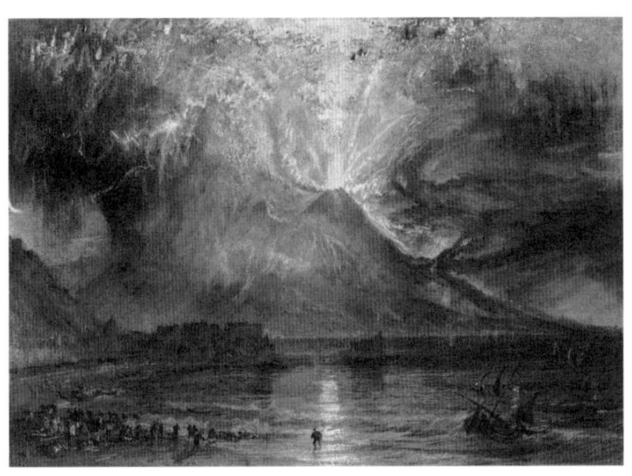

*Vesuvius in Eruption*, c. 1817
Watercolour on paper, 28.6 × 39.7 cm
Yale Center for British Art,
Paul Mellon Collection,
New Haven, Connecticut

## 10 | *The Battle of Trafalgar, 21 October 1805*

Until the early twentieth century, Trafalgar Day was a major celebration on 21 October each year. It was a declaration of the British fleet's supremacy in all Europe. It declined in prominence after 1918 but is still celebrated by the navies of Commonwealth members. When King George IV commissioned a large commemorative picture from Turner, he expected a dignified representation of a resounding, perfect victory. The painter, however, did not always do what was expected of him. He took historical and descriptive liberties, and refused to reconsider.

## 11 | *Regulus*

This picture is both an homage and a challenge. While reflecting veneration of Claude Lorrain, the uncontested master of historical landscape, it makes respectful reference to the Roman hero Regulus. During the First Punic War, Regulus was tortured by the Carthaginians, who cut off his eyelids, left him in the sun and blinded him. The subject of representing blinding brilliance challenged Turner to paint light which hits the picture's subject, viewer and painter all at once.

## 12 | *Scene on the Loire*

Turner never stopped working, frequently juggling several projects at once. He worked in series, planning suites of landscapes and urban scenes, producing oils, prints and books; he did preparatory work using watercolours, gouache and graphite, filling entire sketchbooks with his drawings. His travels took him around Britain and Europe, criss-crossing the landscape to discover new views, stopping and then continuing. The rivers of France captivated him, and in 1826, he spent two weeks aboard a steamboat on the Loire, where he sketched the riverbanks, vessels, cities and more.

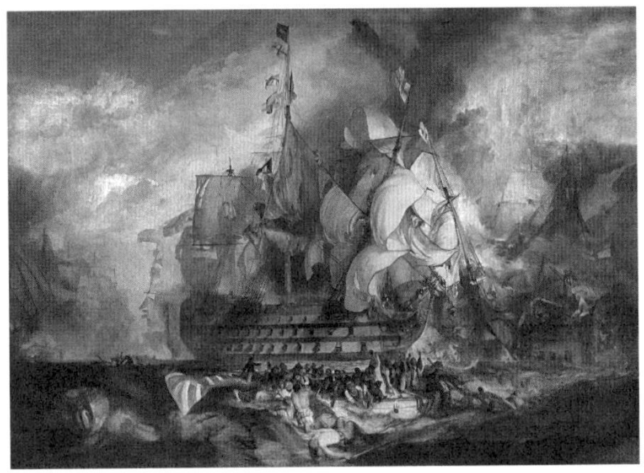

*The Battle of Trafalgar, 21 October 1805,*
1823/1824
Oil on canvas, 261.5 × 368.5 cm
National Maritime Museum,
Greenwich Hospital Collection,
London

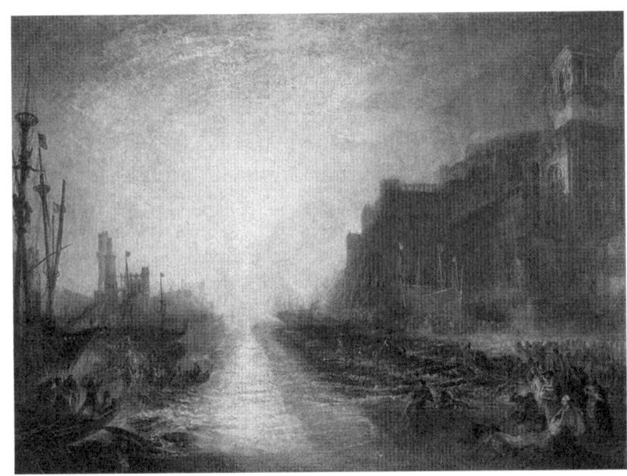

*Regulus*, exhibited in 1828,
reworked and exhibited in 1837
Oil on canvas, 89.5 × 123.8 cm
Tate Britain, London

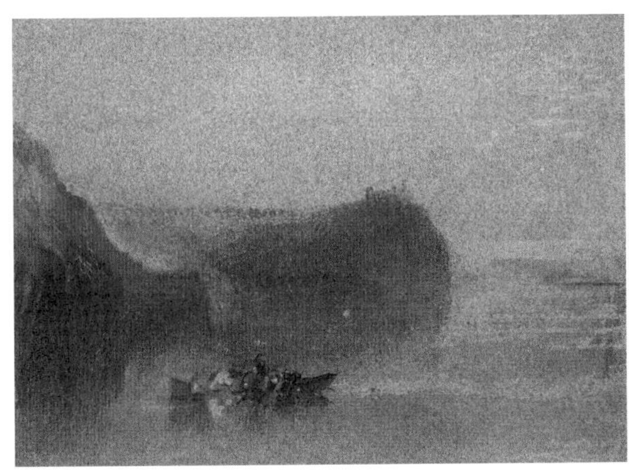

*Scene on the Loire*, c. 1826–1828
Watercolour and gouache on blue
vellum paper, 14 × 19.1 cm
Ashmolean Museum, Oxford

## 13 | *Ulysses Deriding Polyphemus*

Polyphemus, the son of Poseidon and a nymph, appears in book nine of Homer's
*Odyssey*. He inhabits the land of the shepherding, man-eating Cyclopes. Ulysses and
his men journey there and are taken prisoner. To escape, they use several ruses and
put out the eye of the demigod. In Turner's work, the blinding of Polyphemus befits
the luminous blaze of the sky and the sea.

## 14 | *Calais Sands at Low Water: Poissards Collecting Bait*

Turner loved to engage with the Old Masters as well as with those of his contempo-
raries whom he admired. Among them was the painter and watercolourist Richard
Parkes Bonington, who was celebrated for his coastal scenes of Calais, where
his family had settled, and who died in 1828. Turner took up Bonington's vast,
washed-out scenes, deft execution, sparsely rendering figures and adding his own
mark: a flamboyant sunset that transforms the work's tonality.

## 15 | *The Scarlet Sunset: A Town on a River*

While living in London in the autumn of 1870, Claude Monet discovered the
paintings by Turner then exhibited in the National Gallery, and he studied them
very closely. Some years later, *The Scarlet Sunset* seemed to find an echo in Monet's
*Impression, Sunrise*, exhibited in 1874, which gave the movement its name. This is what
the aged Monet was referring to, at some remove, in 1918 in conversation with René
Gimpel: "Back then, I liked Turner very much; today, I like him much less. Why? He
did not give enough form to the colour, of which he used too much."

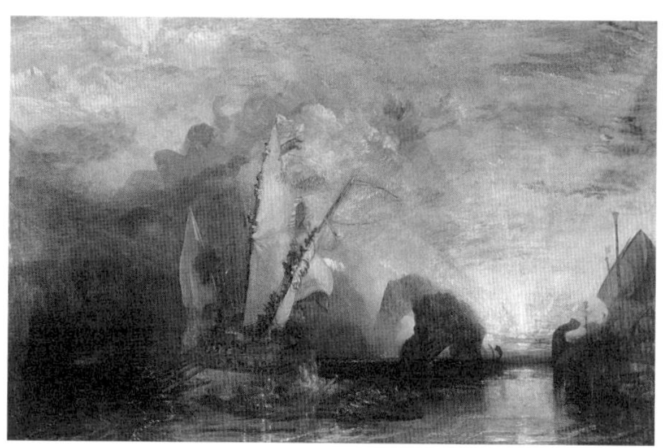

*Ulysses Deriding Polyphemus*,
exhibited in 1829
Oil on canvas, 133 × 203 cm
National Gallery, London

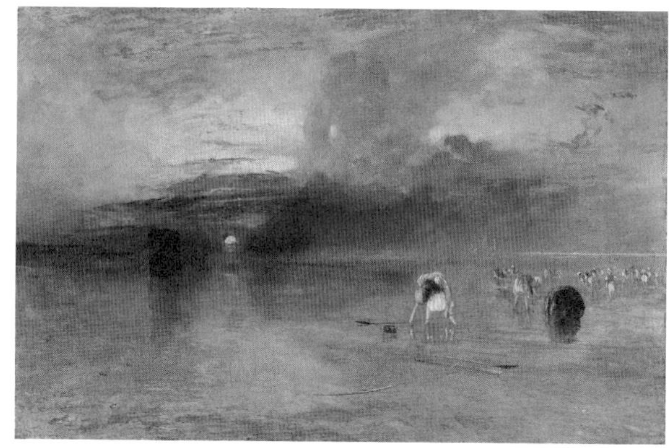

*Calais Sands at Low Water: Poissards
Collecting Bait*, exhibited in 1830
Oil on canvas, 73 × 107 cm
Bury Art Museum, UK

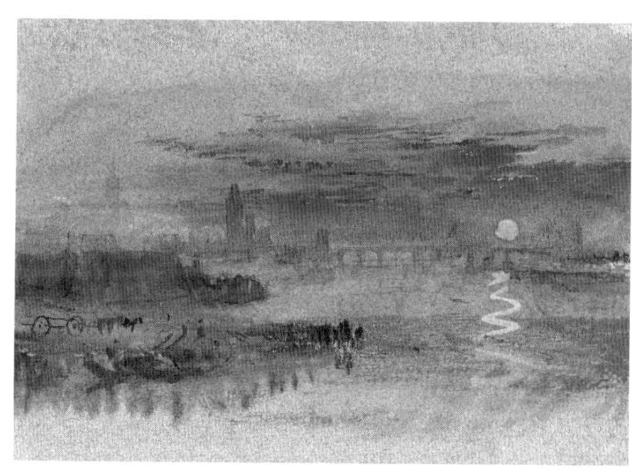

*The Scarlet Sunset: A Town on a River,*
*c.* 1830–1840
Watercolour and gouache on
blue paper, 13.4 × 18.9 cm
Tate Britain, London

**16 | *Dudley, Worcestershire***

In *Modern Painters*, the critic John Ruskin pointed out that Turner particularly excelled at painting fog, because he loved above all else when the land, air and water intermingled: "If you have ever in your life had one opportunity, with your eyes and heart open, of seeing the dew rise from a hill pasture, or the storm gather on a sea-cliff, and if you yet have no feeling for the glorious passages of mingled earth and heaven which Turner calls up before you into breathing tangible being, there is indeed no hope for your apathy, art will never touch you, nor nature inform."

**17 | *River Scene***

"Turner's method was to float-in his broken colours, while the paper was wet, and my late master … told me that he once saw Turner working", recalled the painter James Orrock. "[H]e stretched the paper on boards and, after plunging them into water, he dropped the colours onto the paper while it was wet, making *marblings* and gradations throughout. His completing process was marvellously rapid, for he indicated his masses and incidents, took out half-lights, scraped out high-lights and dragged, hatched and stippled until the design was finished."

**18 | *Venice, from the Porch of Madonna della Salute***

In 1819, Turner stayed in Venice for the first time, and he returned for lengthy stays in 1833 and 1840, working constantly and at all hours. Coming down to the Hotel Europa, near St Mark's Square, he was spotted by one of his British colleagues, the watercolourist William Callow. In *An Autobiography*, Callow recalled, "One evening whilst I was enjoying a cigar in a gondola I saw Turner in another one sketching San Giorgio, brilliantly lit up by the setting sun. I felt quite ashamed of myself idling away my time whilst he was hard at work so late."

26

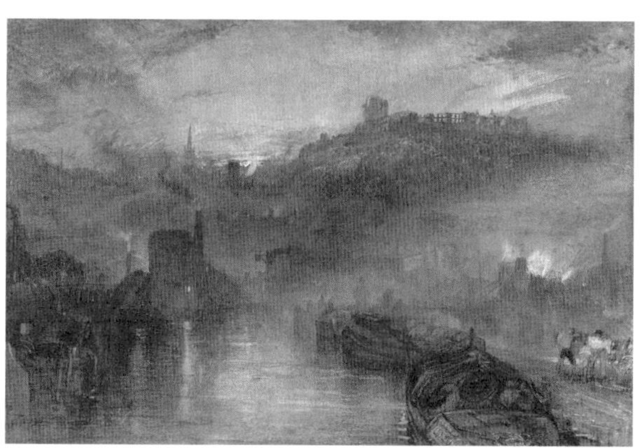

*Dudley, Worcestershire, c. 1832*
Watercolour on paper, 29.3 × 43.2 cm
National Museum, Lady Lever Art
Gallery Collections, Liverpool

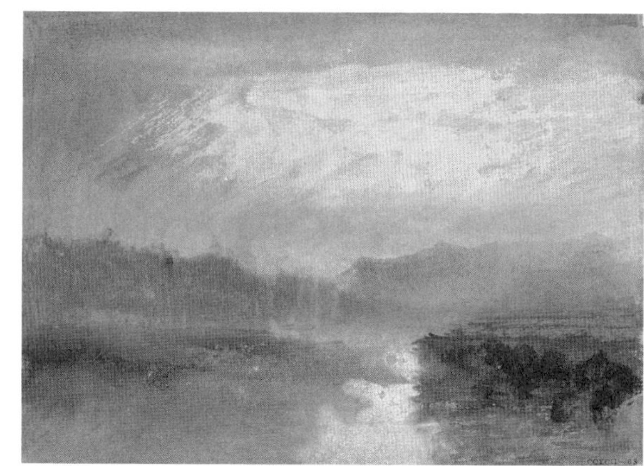

*River Scene*, 1834
Watercolour on paper, 14 × 23 cm
British Museum, London

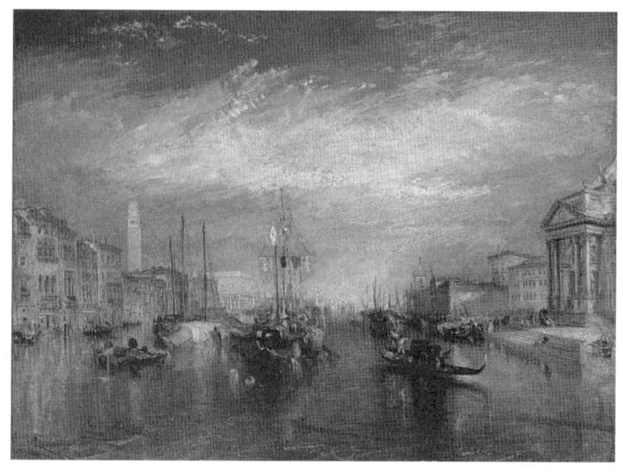

*Venice, from the Porch of Madonna
della Salute*, exhibited in 1835
Oil on canvas, 91.4 × 122.2 cm
Metropolitan Museum of Art,
New York

On this night, accompanied by another painter and students from the Royal Academy, Turner boarded a boat and embarked upon the Thames to see this unimaginable, fascinating, voracious and terrible inferno more closely. His colleague John Constable was positioned on Westminster Bridge. Changing his vantage point several times, Turner produced nine watercolours. Using these, he produced two majestic oils, painted at a feverish rate, which blend observation, innovation and chromatic frenzy. The review in the London *Times* deemed it "one of those masterly productions by which the artist contrives to convey very striking effects with just so much of adherence to nature as prevents one from saying they are merely fanciful."

**21** | *Keelmen Heaving in Coals by Moonlight*

"[T]o a perfectly great manner of painting, or to entirely finished work, a certain degree of indistinctness is indispensable", said John Ruskin of Turner. "The strokes of paint, examined closely, must be confused, odd, incomprehensible … and if we can make anything of them quite out, that part of the drawing is wrong, or incomplete." To Ruskin, this "indistinctness" was part of the painter's mystique, whether he was painting a battle, a storm or an industrial facility.

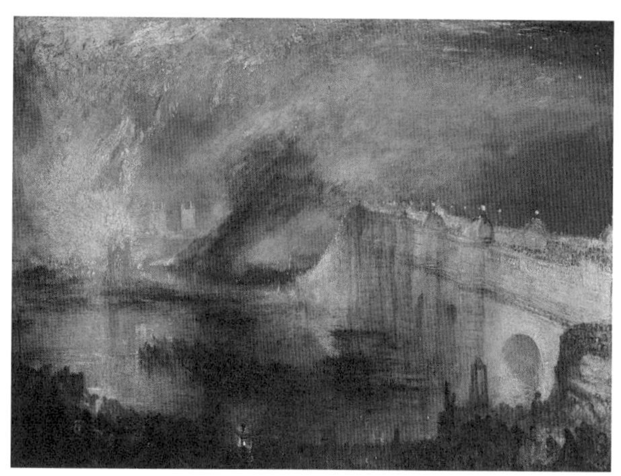

*The Burning of the Houses of Lords
and Commons, October 16, 1834,*
first version exhibited in 1835
Oil on canvas, 92.1 × 123.2 cm
Philadelphia Museum of Art

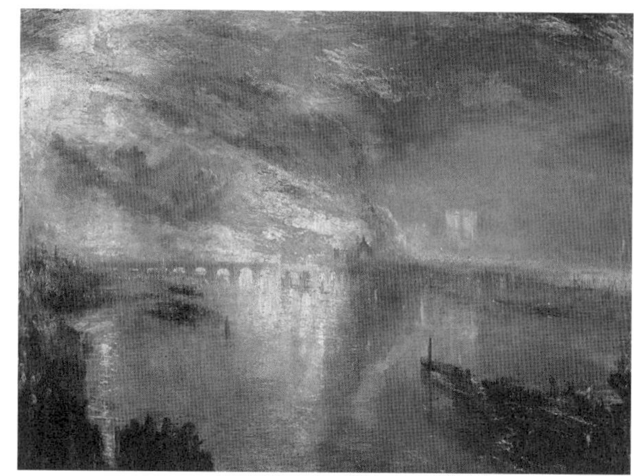

*The Burning of the Houses of Lords
and Commons, October 16, 1834,*
second version exhibited in 1835
Oil on canvas, 92 × 123.2 cm
Cleveland Museum of Art

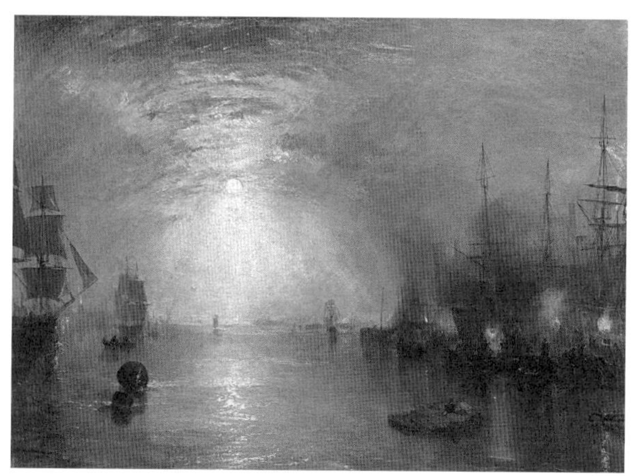

*Keelmen Heaving in Coals
by Moonlight,* 1835
Oil on canvas, 92.3 × 122.8 cm
National Gallery of Art,
Washington, DC

## 22 | *Rome, from Mount Aventine*

"Two months nearly in getting to this 'Terra Pictura', and at work; but the length of time is my own fault", wrote Turner to George Jones on 13 October 1828 from Rome. The "Terra Pictura" he was referring to was Italy, Rome: the idealised, academic vision of antiquity that the painter had built up since his training, since his "apprenticeship" with the Old Masters. Turner discovered the real Rome in 1819 and returned there some ten years later. Surely he was not too overcome; surely he was disappointed after having dreamed of it so much.

## 23 | *A Sailing Boat off Deal*

Though the great traveller Turner toured the length and breadth of Europe, he was no stranger to his own country. He began to make study visits in Britain in the late eighteenth century, and he resided at Brentford, then Margate. He also worked in Deal, a fishing port between Ramsgate and Dover, where he created oil paintings and many sketches.

## 24 | *Landscape with a River and a Bay in the Distance*

When Joris-Karl Huysmans discovered Turner's art in Paris – where this painting depicting the Severn estuary, on the English-Welsh border, was exhibited – he was stunned. "The viewer is faced with an absolute riot of rose and burnt sienna, of blue and white, rubbed with a cloth, here in circles and there running in a straight line or bifurcating in long zigzags", he wrote in 1889. "It is like a print that has been swept with a soft piece of bread, or a mass of delicate colours spread out with water on a sheet of paper that is folded, then scraped strenuously with a brush."

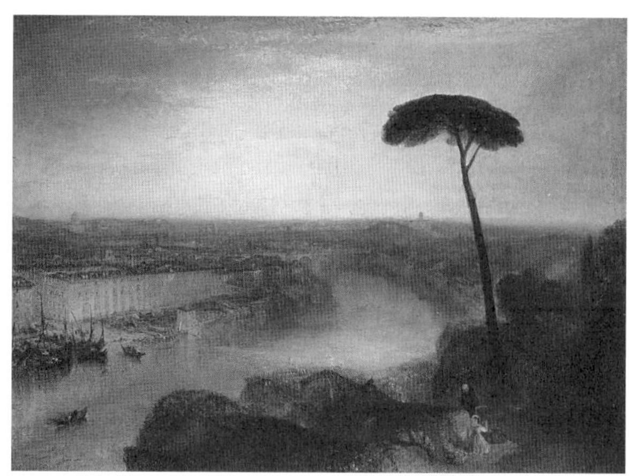

*Rome, from Mount Aventine*, 1835
Oil on canvas, 92.7 × 125.7 cm
Private collection

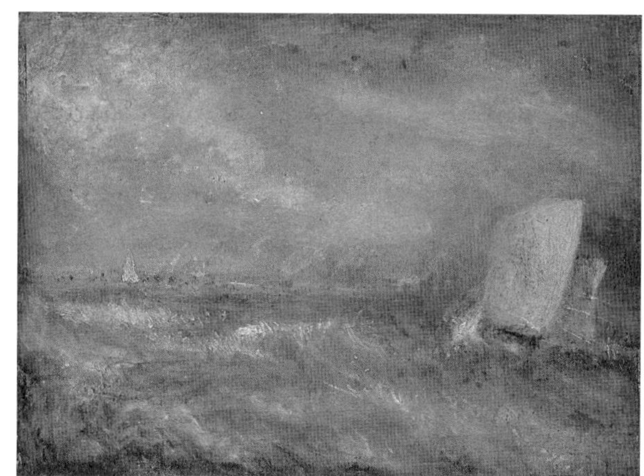

*A Sailing Boat off Deal*, c. 1835–1845
Oil on cardboard, 22.6 × 30.3 cm
National Museum Wales, Cardiff

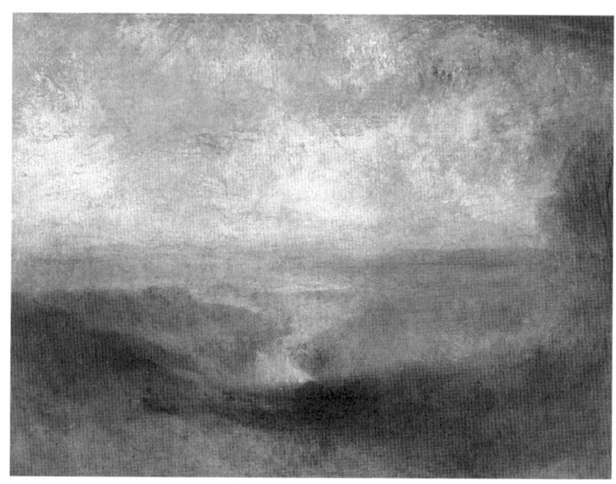

*Landscape with a River and a Bay in
the Distance, unfinished*, c. 1835–1845
Oil on canvas, 94 × 124 cm
Louvre, Paris

Light is the business of painters. Of course, it is also the business of scientists. Turner was enthusiastic about research performed in the late eighteenth century, and in the early nineteenth century he considered himself up-to-date on a full range of topics from astronomy to optics. He attended conferences, and in the 1820s, through his acquaintance with the Scottish physician David Brewster (the inventor of the kaleidoscope), he surely encountered the wave theory of light established by Augustin Fresnel. Knowing that light is defined by undulation, vibration and diffraction could not help but affect how he painted.

**26 and 27 |** *Castle on Height near Geneva*
       *Valley of Aosta: Snowstorm, Avalanche and Thunderstorm*

"In Turner's genius there is something magical and enigmatic which singularly repels reality", said the Parisian art review *L'Artiste* in 1833. "Give Turner Wales, England, the Loire, the Pyrenees, the Alps, give him the Colosseum or the Doge's Palace, and he will shower all these subjects with grandeur and grace. Between subjects that are least alike, he will establish a mysterious kinship." Moving from watercolour to oil, the artist observed, noticed, studied, isolated, recomposed, balanced, upset, cut, added, accentuated and so on.

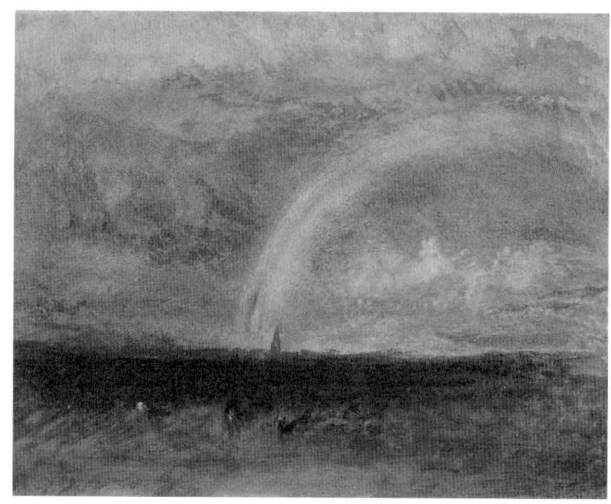

*The Rainbow, c.* 1835–1845
Watercolour on paper, 23.9 × 30 cm
National Museum Wales, Cardiff

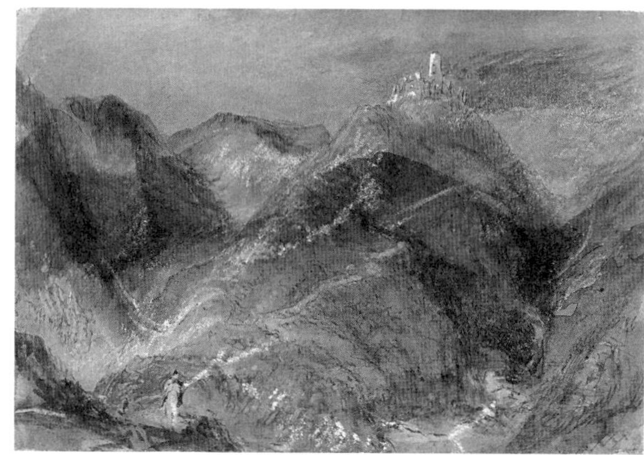

*Castle on Height near Geneva,* 1836
Watercolour and graphite on
white vellum paper, 16 × 23.4 cm
Art Institute of Chicago

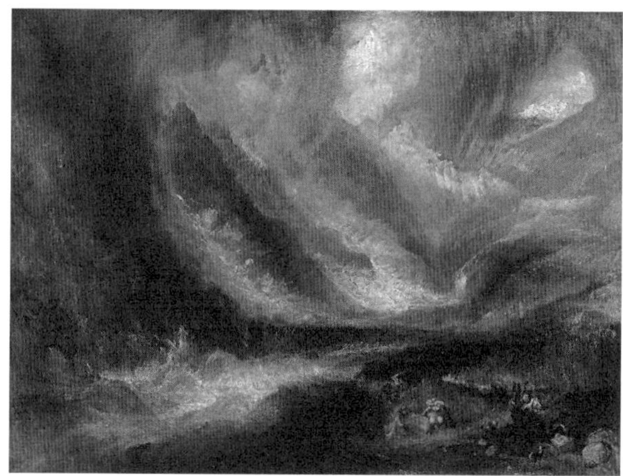

*Valley of Aosta: Snowstorm, Avalanche
and Thunderstorm,* 1836/1837
Oil on canvas, 92.2 × 123 cm
Art Institute of Chicago

**28 | *Fishing Boats with Hucksters Bargaining for Fish***

Turner chose influences from all the artistic traditions, and the Dutch artists of the seventeenth century were prominent in that pantheon. Before a print from a Dutch seascape painter, he could well have declared, "Ah! This made me into a painter!" His predecessors made it possible for him to gain confidence, freedom and daring in the face of rigid academia. Like them, he told no story in this painting. He delivered no message, instead endeavouring to evoke the daily labour of fishers of the sea.

**29 | *The Fighting Temeraire, Tugged to Her Last Berth to Be Broken Up***

"My Darling" was Turner's name for this painting, whose tragic power pays tribute to the *Fighting Temeraire*. After taking part in the Battle of Trafalgar in 1805, the warship was then used as a prison ship and finally was sold and dismasted in 1838. Dethroned but proud behind the steam tugboat, she represents the sadness of past glory, the end of a world, the cruelty of history. "In this scene, there is something that affects us as much as the decline of a man", wrote a member of the press about this work, which was destined for immense popularity.

**30 | *The Rape of Proserpine***

Proserpine, the daughter of Ceres and Jupiter, was both the Roman goddess of spring and the queen of the underworld. After abducting her as she picked violets with companions, Pluto married her and installed her as ruler of the dead. Her desperate and furious mother, Ceres, embarked on a search for her, and decided to allow the crops to die in retaliation. Proserpine divided her time between earth, in spring and summer, and the underworld, in autumn and winter. Her abduction became the foundational myth behind the cycle of seasons.

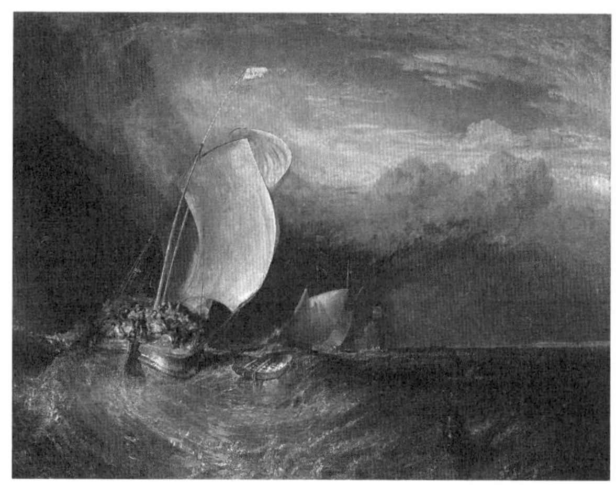

*Fishing Boats with Hucksters Bargaining
for Fish*, 1837/1838
Oil on canvas, 174.5 × 224.9 cm
Art Institute of Chicago

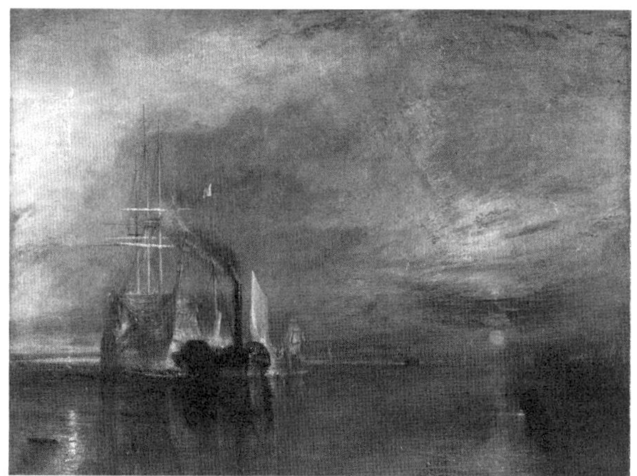

*The Fighting Temeraire, Tugged to
Her Last Berth to Be Broken Up*,
exhibited in 1839
Oil on canvas, 90.7 × 121.6 cm
National Gallery, London

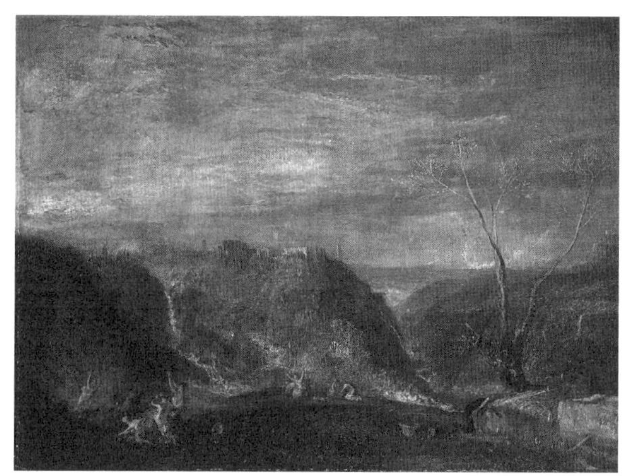

*The Rape of Proserpine*, 1839
Oil on canvas, 92.6 × 123.7 cm
National Gallery of Art,
Washington, DC

**31 and 32 | *Modern Rome – Campo Vaccino***
**    *Venice, the Bridge of Sighs***

Turner preferred Venice, the gleaming city of light and of marvels, to Rome, the city where one studied the past, archaeology and history. He made his choice early on, and his works show it often. In Rome, he depicted the Forum from the Capitoline Hill, depicting relics of antiquity, the Renaissance and the Baroque. In Venice, he depicted processions, small boats and gondolas against an architectural backdrop, in the manner of opera scenery. Exhibitions of his Venetian paintings in the 1830s and 1840s were met with success.

**33 | *View off Margate, Evening***

In certain paintings (which may be just studies for larger works) there is no narrative pretext, even though the elements for it are in place: a woman with children, a small boat on the beach, a light sailboat, a vessel in the distance. Emphasis is placed on the paint itself, which no longer represents the sea foam or the clouds; it *is* the sea foam and the clouds.

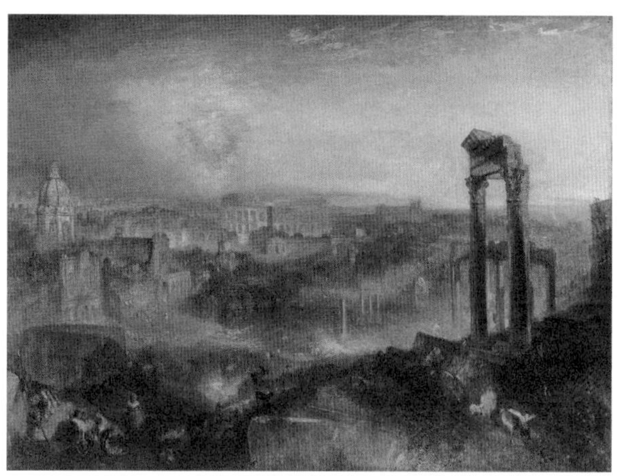

*Modern Rome – Campo Vaccino*, 1839
Oil on canvas, 91.8 × 122.6 cm
J. Paul Getty Museum, Los Angeles

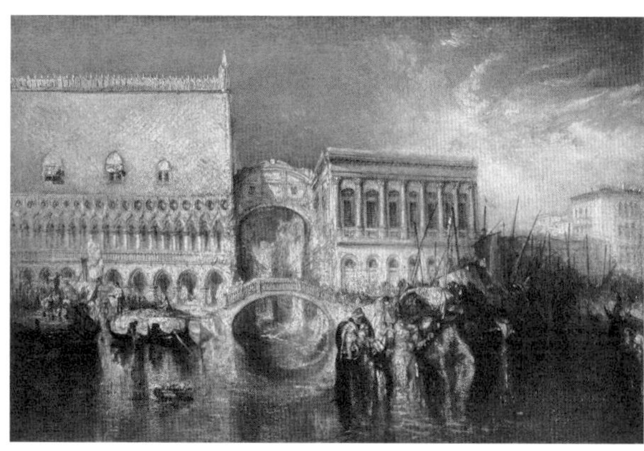

*Venice, the Bridge of Sighs*, 1840
Oil on canvas, 68.6 × 91.4 cm
Tate Britain, London

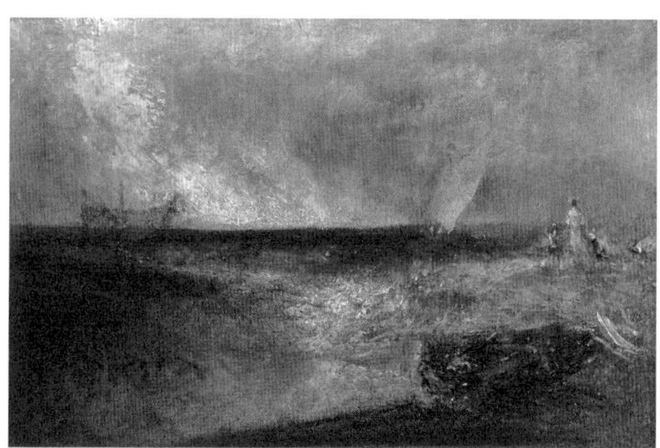

*View off Margate, Evening, c.* 1840
Oil on canvas, 32.1 × 48.9 cm
Clark Art Institute, Williamstown,
Massachusetts

**34 | *Slave Ship (Slavers Throwing Overboard the Dead and Dying, Typhoon Coming On)***

The sea is coloured red not from a radiant incandescence but from the blood of Black slaves thrown overboard. Turner exhibited this work, which was doubtless inspired by an event that occurred in the late eighteenth century, at an abolitionists' conference, and he accompanied it with a poem that he had written. Though mocked by some for its indistinctness, its extravagant colours and his excessive use of the palette knife, the work was defended by others. John Ruskin, the painting's first owner, admired its power, its daring and its sense of the sublime.

**35 | *Rockets and Blue Lights (Close at Hand) to Warn Steamboats of Shoal Water***

Although Turner divided critics, writers and artists both during his life and after his death, they all attested to his passion. "Lawrence, Turner, Reynolds and generally speaking, all the great English painters have this defect of exaggeration, especially in the general effect, a fault that prevents them from being ranked among the great masters", wrote Eugène Delacroix in his *Journal* on 8 February 1860. "The cloudy and variable skies of their country lead them to produce these extravagant effects, these sudden contrasts of light and darkness, but they greatly exaggerate them, revealing defects caused by fashion or personal bias that speak louder than their fine qualities."

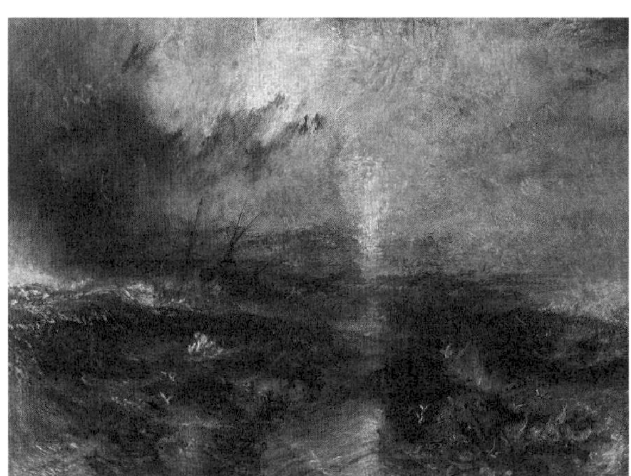

*Slave Ship (Slavers Throwing Overboard
the Dead and Dying, Typhoon Coming On)*,
exhibited in 1840
Oil on canvas, 91 × 138 cm
Museum of Fine Arts, Boston

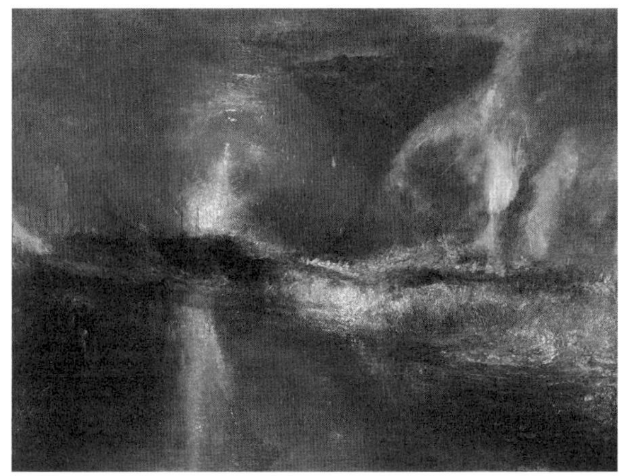

*Rockets and Blue Lights (Close at Hand)
to Warn Steamboats of Shoal Water*, 1840
Oil on canvas, 92.1 × 122.2 cm
Clark Art Institute, Williamstown,
Massachusetts

Seemingly unnatural colours in landscapes – here purple, there too much yellow – is one of the criticisms often levied against Turner. So are hazy technique and a lack of precision when rendering settings. "We suppose we see the ground under our feet clearly", wrote the critic John Ruskin about Turner, "but if we try to number its grains of dust, we shall find that it is as full of confusion and doubtful form as anything else; so that there is literally no point of clear sight, and there never can be."

**38 |** *Dawn after the Wreck*

Turner depicted many shipwrecks. More uncommon are the scenes showing the aftermath, when the calm returns, fragile and shaken by the recent upheaval. All that is left is a dog, alone, howling furiously, to draw our gaze to the right, towards a shore where everything – and everyone – has disappeared. We are mesmerised, held by compassion. Twenty years later, in his Quinta del Sordo, or Villa of the Deaf Man, Francisco Goya painted the head of a dog struggling to emerge from a mass of paint, creating immediate unease.

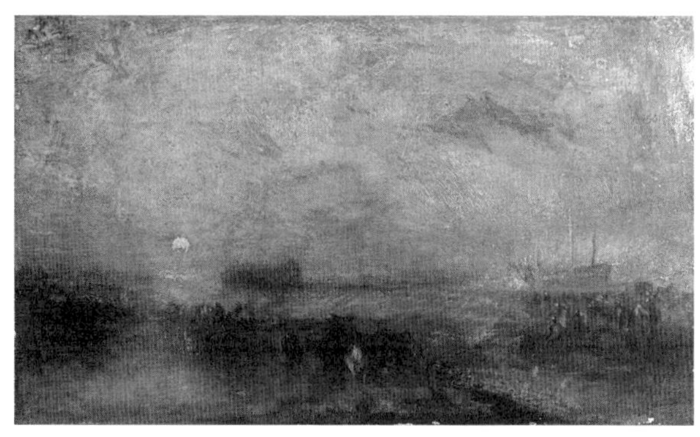

*The Morning after the Storm*, 1840–1845
Oil on canvas, 32.6 × 54.4 cm
National Museum Wales, Cardiff

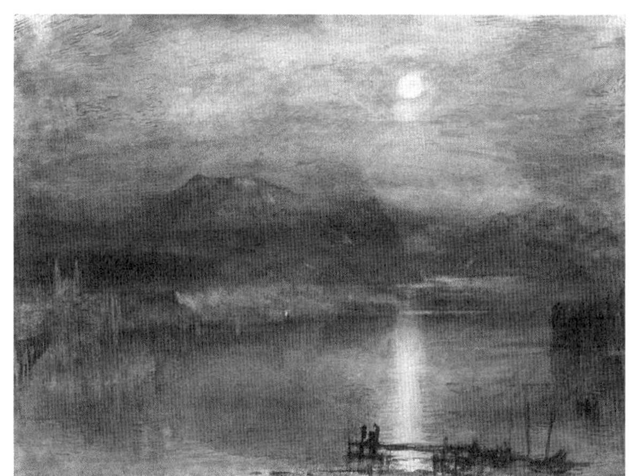

*Moonlight on Lake Lucerne with the Rigi
in the Distance*, c. 1841
Watercolour and gouache on paper,
22.9 × 30.6 cm
Whitworth Art Gallery,
Manchester University, Manchester

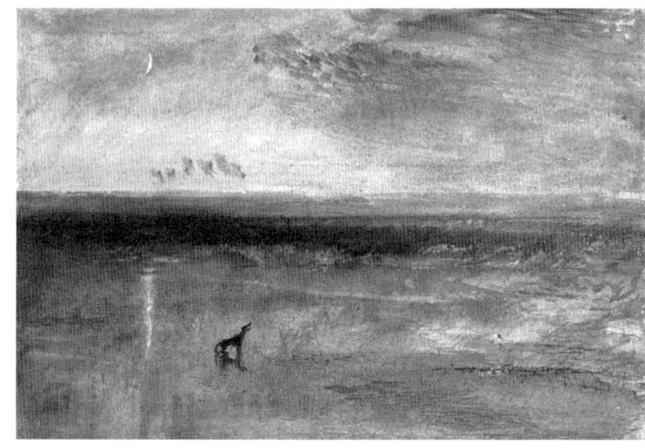

*Dawn after the Wreck*, c. 1841
Watercolour and gouache on paper,
24.5 × 36.2 cm
Courtauld Institute Galleries, London

**39 and 40 |** *The Blue Rigi, Sunrise*
    *The Lake of Zug*

Turner was passionate about Switzerland's lakes and mountains, which he depicted
in a series of watercolours in the early 1840s. Most of these were commissions, or a
kind of sample to show to patrons: the artist would use them to show the setting, the
point of view or the time of day he had selected, the colours, the absence or presence
of human figures, and so on; and when the customer had decided, Turner would
begin working to the specified size, technique and degree of finishing. For the Rigi,
the view was from the shore of Lake Lucerne; for the Lake of Zug, the dawn was
tinged with blue.

**41 |** *Snow Storm – Steam-Boat off a Harbour's Mouth*

The artist and traveller Turner undoubtably often found himself in peril on the road,
in the sea, in the mountains and elsewhere. What he experienced, he painted, and
what he painted, he had experienced, as he asserted in this work's full title – whether
it was true or not. A review published in the *Athenaeum* on 14 May 1842, however,
criticized him for showing nothing: "This gentleman has, on former occasions,
chosen to paint with cream, or chocolate, yolk of egg, or currant jelly, – here he uses
his whole array of kitchen stuff. Where the steam-boat is – where the harbour begins,
or where it ends – which are the signals, and which the author in the *Ariel* … are
matters past our finding out."

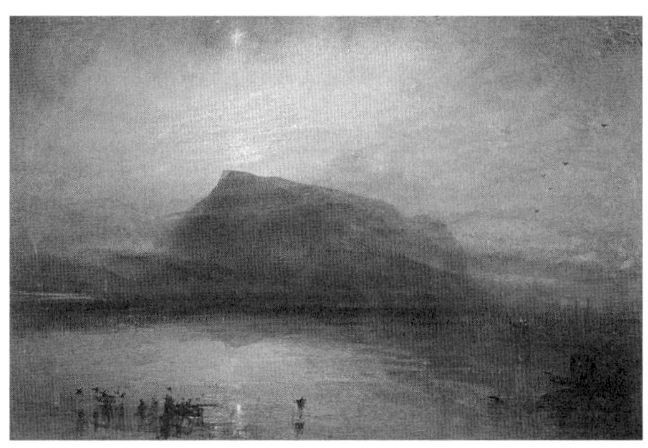

*The Blue Rigi, Sunrise*, 1842
Watercolour on paper, 29.7 × 45 cm
Tate Britain, London

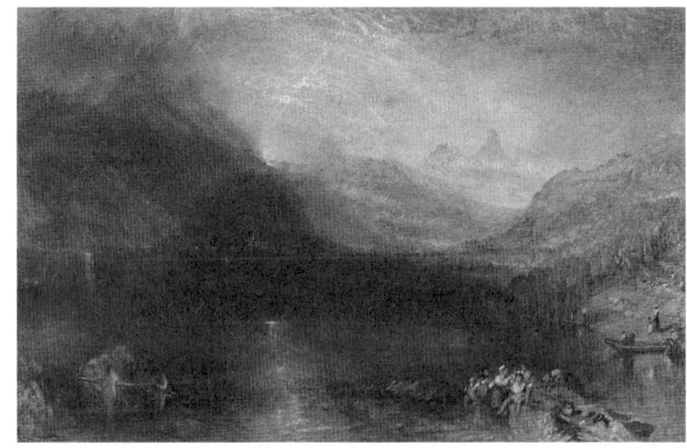

*The Lake of Zug*, 1843
Watercolour and graphite on paper,
29.8 × 46.6 cm
Metropolitan Museum of Art,
New York

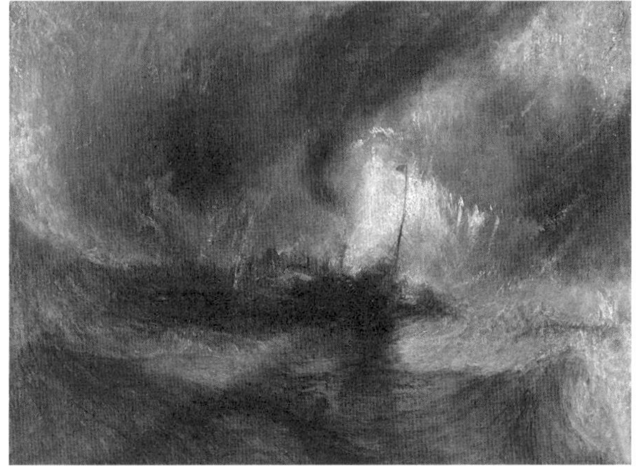

*Snow Storm – Steam-Boat off a
Harbour's Mouth Making Signals in
Shallow Water, and Going by the Lead.
The Author Was in this Storm on the
Night the "Ariel" Left Harwich*,
exhibited in 1842
Oil on canvas, 91.4 × 121.9 cm
Tate Britain, London

**42 |** *Light and Colour (Goethe's Theory) – The Morning after the Deluge –*
*Moses Writing the Book of Genesis*

Turner was a great painter, and he was also a great reader of travelogues, collections
of poetry, writings on art, treatises on perspective and colour, old and contemporary
debates on aesthetics, and more. In 1840, Goethe's *Theory of Colours* had just been
translated into English. Turner read it, made notes and used it as the subject of one
of his paintings, creating a dialogue between theoretician and artist – each in his
own domain.

**43 |** *Rain, Steam, and Speed – The Great Western Railway*

This picture of noise and furore, impasto and erasures, was received well at the Royal
Academy. Is it a recollection of how Turner experienced speed? Or does it evoke the
thunderous meeting between the British Industrial Revolution of the 1840s (a metal
viaduct, a steam locomotive) and the remnants of an old world in the process of
disappearing (a farm landscape, a stone bridge and a leaping hare in the foreground)?

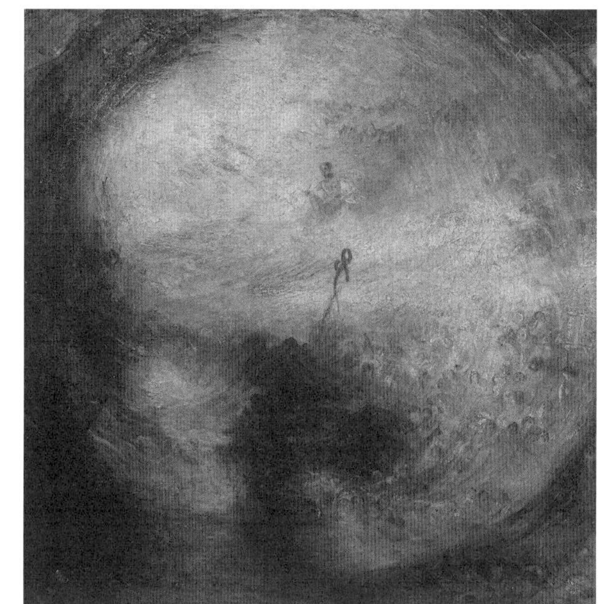

*Light and Colour (Goethe's Theory) –*
*The Morning after the Deluge –*
*Moses Writing the Book of Genesis,* 1843
Oil on canvas, 78 × 78 cm
Tate Britain, London

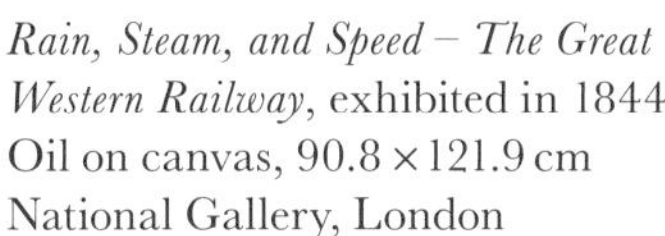

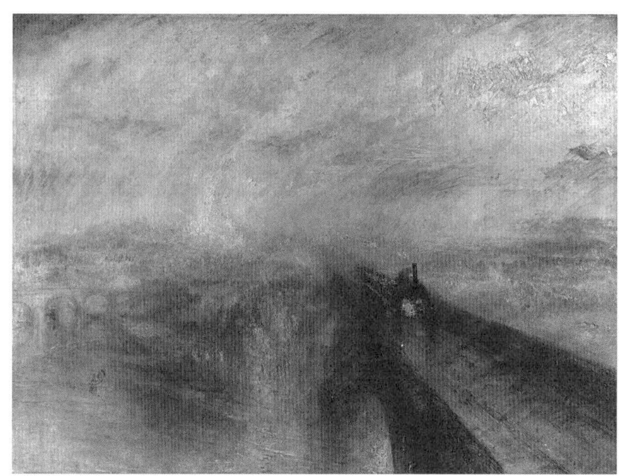

*Rain, Steam, and Speed – The Great*
*Western Railway,* exhibited in 1844
Oil on canvas, 90.8 × 121.9 cm
National Gallery, London

**44 and 45** | *Approach to Venice*
        *Going to the Ball (San Martino)*

There was Venice as Turner knew it, in the eighteenth century, the Venice of Cana-
letto and Francesco Guardi; then, there is the Venice of Richard Parkes Bonington
in the early nineteenth century and the Venice to come, the early-twentieth-century
Venice, the Venice of Claude Monet. In oil or watercolour, it is a familiar Venice,
powerful and proud of its monuments (see numbers 18 and 32), or a dreamlike Venice,
overtaken by fog coloured gold or by a glow from which figures emerge – a city
consumed by the very materiality of the painting.

**46** | *The Wreck Buoy*

On the Royal Academy's varnishing days, people would plan ahead to see the
veritable performances that Turner would put on. On the spot, in public, he would
retouch his paintings that were ready to be exhibited. Armed with his little box of
paints and his instruments, he would spread, scrape, add some white here, add a final
detail there or add to the foreground a touch of red (which might become a wreck
buoy) to draw the eye, reinforce depth or shake up the balance of a composition.
"He used rather short brushes, a very messy palette, and, standing very close up to
the canvas, appeared to paint with his eyes and nose as well as his hand", recounted
G. D. Leslie. "Of course, he repeatedly walked back to study the effect."

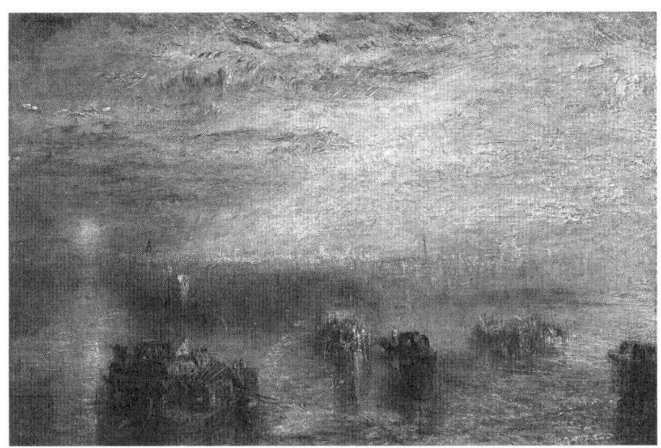

*Approach to Venice*, 1844
Oil on canvas, 62 × 94 cm
National Gallery of Art,
Washington, DC

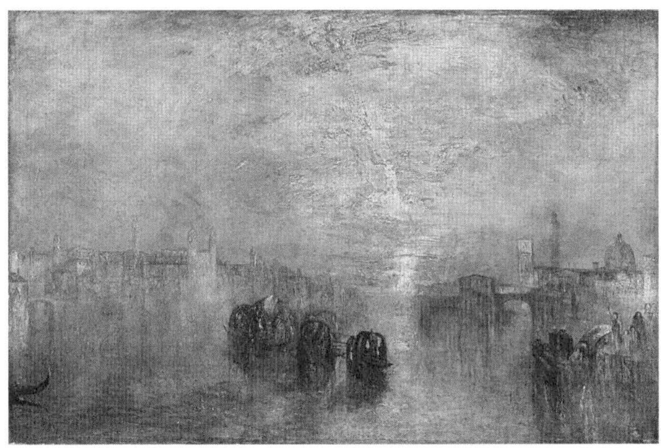

*Going to the Ball (San Martino)*,
exhibited in 1846
Oil on canvas, 61.6 × 92.4 cm
Tate Britain, London

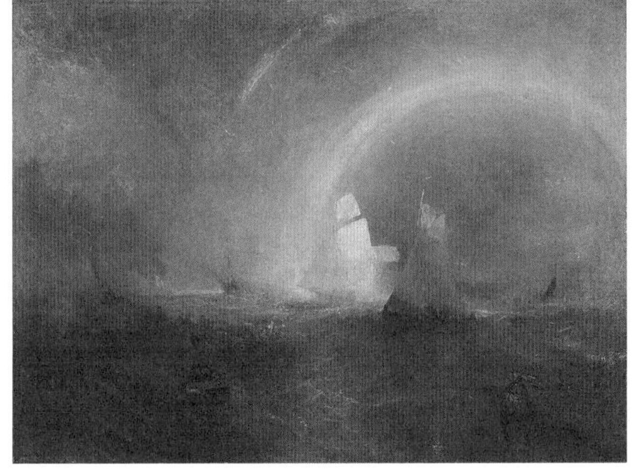

*The Wreck Buoy*, *c.* 1849
Oil on canvas, 92.7 × 123.2 cm
Walker Art Gallery,
National Museum, Liverpool

*Photographic Credits*

Alamy: Artchives/Alamy: pp. 1, 11, 15; AIFA Visuals/Alamy: p. 6; Ian Dagnall/Alamy: p. 10; Heritage Image Partnership Ltd/Alamy: p. 25; Artiz/Alamy: p. 32; World History Archive/Alamy: p. 41; Picture Art Collection/Alamy: p. 42; Picture Art Collection/Alamy: p. 45

Art Institute of Chicago: Gift of Dorothy Braude Edinburg to the Harry B. and Bessie K. Braude Memorial Collection: p. 26; Frederick T. Haskell Collection: p. 27; Mr. and Mrs. W. W. Kimball Collection: p. 30

Bridgeman Images: pp. 9, 17, 23, 29, 36, 43; Photo © Agnew's, London: p. 4; Photo © Derek Bayes: pp. 8, 13; © Ashmolean Museum: p. 12; © Bury Art Museum & Sculpture Centre: p. 14; © National Museums Liverpool: pp. 16, 46; Bequest of John L. Severance: p. 20; © Photo Josse: p. 24; © Museum of Fine Arts, Boston/Henry Lillie Pierce Fund: p. 34; © Whitworth Art Gallery © The Whitworth, The University of Manchester: p. 37; © Courtauld Gallery: p. 38; Photo © Agnew's, London: p. 39 and cover

Indianapolis Museum of Art: p. 3

J. Paul Getty Museum: pp. 2, 31

National Gallery of Art, Washington, DC: Corcoran Collection (William A. Clark Collection): p. 5; Widener Collection: p. 21; Gift of Mrs. Watson B. Dickerman: p. 30; Andrew W. Mellon Collection: p. 44

Philadelphia Museum of Art/The John Howard McFadden Collection, 1928: p. 19

Clark Art Institute, Williamstown, Massachusetts: Gift of the Manton Art Foundation in memory of Sir Edwin and Lady Manton, 2007: p. 33; Acquired by Sterling and Francine Clark, 1932: p. 35

Metropolitan Museum of Art, New York: Bequest of Cornelius Vanderbilt, 1899: p. 18; Marquand Fund, 1959: p. 40

Yale Center for British Art, Paul Mellon Collection: p. 7

© Prestel Verlag, Munich · London · New York, 2025
A member of Penguin Random House Verlagsgruppe GmbH
Neumarkter Strasse 28 · 81673 Munich

The publisher expressly reserves the right to exploit the copyrighted content of this work for the purposes of text and data mining in accordance with Section 44b of the German Copyright Act (UrhG), based on the European Digital Single Market Directive. Any unauthorized use is an infringement of copyright and is hereby prohibited.

A CIP catalogue record for this book is available from the British Library.

The French original edition was published by Éditions Hazan as *Turner: Coffret l'essentiel.*

© Editions Hazan, 2021

Translation
Richard N. Block

Copy-editing
Tas Skorupa

Production
Martina Effaga

Typesetting
Sieveking Agentur, Munich

Repro
Litho Art New, Turin, Italy

Printing and binding
Toppan Leefung Printing

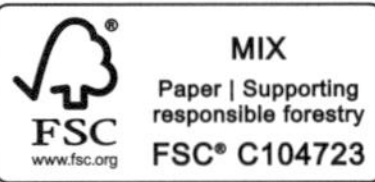

Penguin Random House Verlagsgruppe
FSC® N001967

Printed in China

ISBN 978-3-7913-7780-3
www.prestel.com